WHILE SHEPHERDS WASHED THEIR SOCKS

David Orme lives in Winchester and is the author of a wide range of poetry books, textbooks and picture books for children. When he is not writing he visits schools, performing poetry and running poetry workshops and encouraging children and teachers to enjoy poetry.

Giles Pilbrow draws cartoons weekly for the *Sunday Times*, and regularly for *Private Eye* and the *Spectator* amongst others. He has written for and produced numerous series of *Spitting Image* and *The Big Breakfast*. He has also written and illustrated four other children's books.

Other books by David Orme

'ERE WE GO!
Football Poems

YOU'LL NEVER WALK ALONE
More Football Poems

WE WAS ROBBED
Yet More Football Poems

DRACULA'S AUNTIE RUTHLESS
and other Petrifying Poems

SNOGGERS
Slap 'n' Tickle Poems

NOTHING TASTES QUITE LIKE A GERBIL
and other Vile Verses

WHILE SHEPHERDS WASHED THEIR SOCKS

and other poems
chosen by David Orme

Illustrated by
Giles Pilbrow

MACMILLAN CHILDREN'S BOOKS

First published 1997 by
Macmillan Children's Books
a division of Macmillan Publishers Ltd
25 Eccleston Place London SW1W 9NF
and Basingstoke

Associated companies throughout the world

ISBN 0 330 35335 7

1 3 5 7 9 8 6 4 2

A CIP catalogue record for this book is available from the British Library.

Typeset by Macmillan Children's Books
Printed by Mackays of Chatham Plc

For Joseph Sale

A Christmas Present

CONTENTS

Christmas Worm 1

Out of the cracker
with a flash and a squirm:
'Merry Christmas! It's me again!'
cried the worm.

Tony Mitton

Topsy-Turvy Christmas

No more boring Christmases
Be original instead:
Hang hot water bottles on the tree
Put holly in the bed!

Hide the Christmas presents
Until Midsummer's Day.
Keep the wrapping paper
And throw the gifts away.

Hang the pudding in the hall
And eat the mistletoe.
It's poisonous as anything
But what a way to go!

Put the trifle down the toilet
Pour the brandy on the mat
Serve the mince pies up with gravy
Give the turkey to the cat!

No more boring Christmases
It's time to make a break
Eat the Christmas crackers
And pull the Christmas cake!

Put the tinsel in the dustbin
Hang the rubbish on the wall
Make confetti with the Christmas cards
And have a free-for-all!

Rex Andrews

Father Christmas is Asleep

Father Christmas is asleep on his sled
With dreams full of chimneys alive in his head;
But there's no one can do this job instead
Of Father Christmas – who's asleep on his sled.

Father Christmas is asleep on his sled.
Reindeers are stamping, waiting to be fed
And present-packers are still tucked up in bed!
But Father Christmaz is asleep on his sled . . .

Father Christmaz is azleep on his sled.
There's sacks full of gifts in the Big Goody Shed
And hundreds of letters still to be read
By Father Chriztmaz – who's asleep on his zled.

Father Chriztmaz is azleep on hiz sled.
'Wake him up in good time!' Mrs Christmas had said.
But Ned didn't, Fred didn't and neither did Ted,
Zo Father Zizztmazz iz ztill azleep on hiz zled.

Trevor Millum

Christmas Worm 2

Christmas is coming
and the worm is getting fat.
'Watch out, Santa,
or you'll squash her flat.'

Tony Mitton

Santa's Sad Sack

When Santa reached
inside his sack,
he pulled out a grubby
anorak,

a smelly welly,
some dirty socks
and a mangled plastic
sandwich box.

'Oh no . . .' said Santa,
beginning to sag.
'I've brought the Gnomes'
Lost Property Bag!'

Tony Mitton

Christmas Eve Trip

If you hear a creak at Christmas
in the middle of the night,
it'll just be Santa searching
to find your toilet light.

For after flying round the world
and one sherry too many,
Santa will always need to stop
and spend a little penny.

Andrew Collett

Enough Stuff

Too much turkey,
Too much pud.
I'm not feeling
Very good.

Too much stuffing,
Too much pop.
My stomach's bursting.
I'm going to drop.

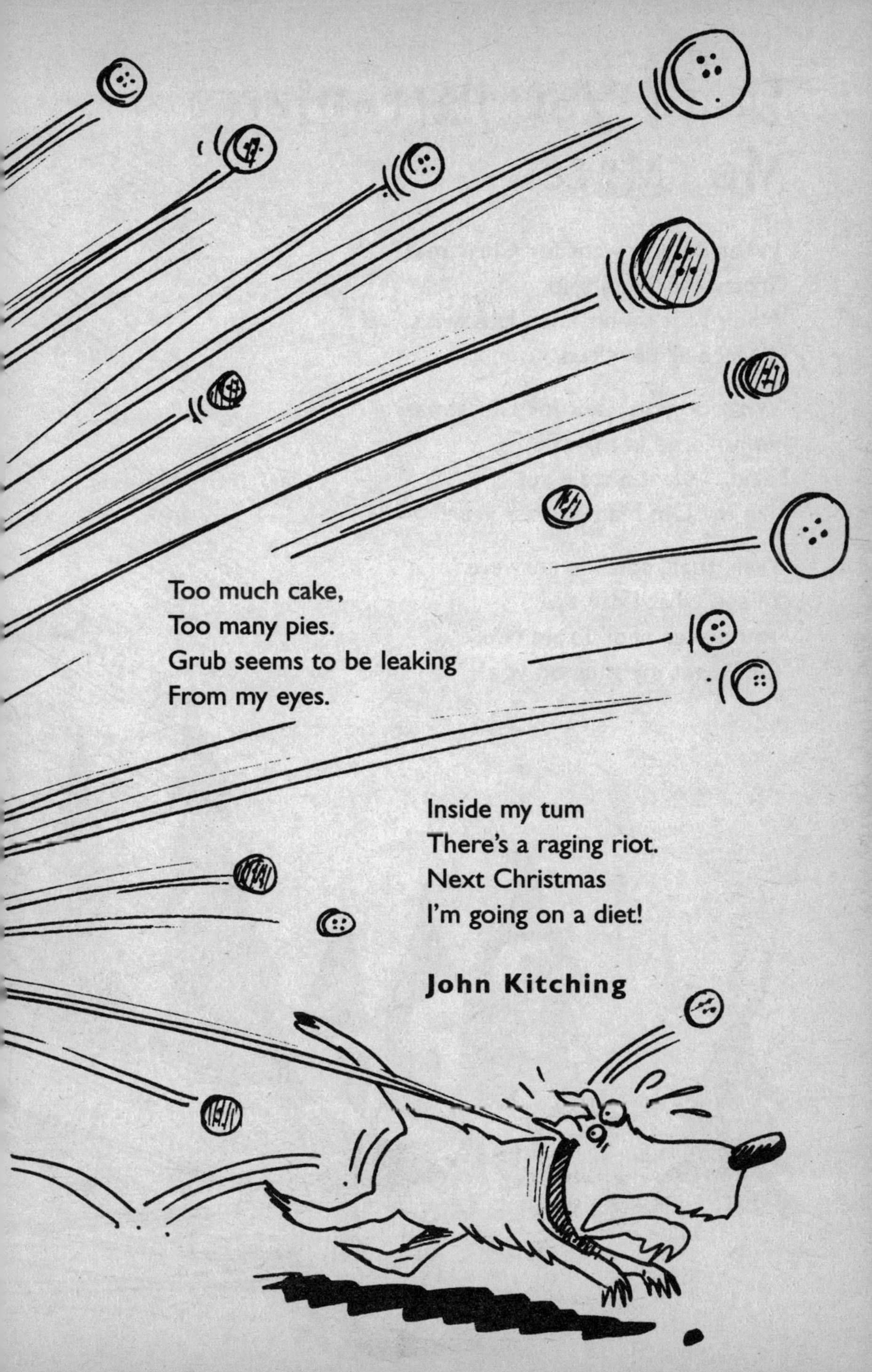

Too much cake,
Too many pies.
Grub seems to be leaking
From my eyes.

Inside my tum
There's a raging riot.
Next Christmas
I'm going on a diet!

John Kitching

Don't You Patronize Me, Mate

'What do you want for Christmas?'
Grotty old Santa said
When I sat on his knee in Lewis's,
His face all fiery red.

'What do you want for Christmas?'
He hollered in my ear.
I said, 'I want a train set
Like my Old Man got last year!'

'Well, then, son,' he answered,
'I'll see what I can do.'
'You better had!' I told him.
'Or I'll get my gang on you!

'They'll marmalize your reindeer,
Put holes in your sack,
Whoosh rockets up the chimbley
So's you won't be coming back!'

He rapped me on my bobble hat,
He tweaked me by the ear,
He gave me a plastic dinosaur
And called me *Little Dear*!

That night I wrote this letter
On behalf of all the gang:
'Look, Mister, we have rockets
That go off with a bang!

'And remember about the train set,
Make sure it's in the sack . . .
Oh, and bring along a million pound
If you want your reindeer back!'

Matt Simpson

The Decorated Toilet

The Smith family next door to us
at number twenty-two
decided, for Christmas day,
to decorate their loo.

They planted trees inside the pot
and hung chocolates from the chain,
they tied baubles to ballcocks
and flushed fairies down the drain.

They tied tinsel onto the tank
and put presents round the bowl,
they even found a special
Christmas toilet roll.

Then, suddenly, they all stood still
and held their heads down low,
for, with a decorated toilet,
there was nowhere for them to *go*.

Which is the reason the Smith family
from number twenty-two,
came round to us on Christmas day
to try and use our loo.

Andrew Collett

Merrily On High

Santa's trudging –
rooftop snow.

Hidden chimney . . .

'Ho Ho H
O
o
o
o
o
!'

Mike Johnson

Mistletoe Madness

A curse on drooping mistletoe
And all that sloppiness below;
Lipsticked pouts from Auntie Millie,
Whiskery hugs with Uncle Billy,
And then the part I really hate,
They make me kiss my sister Kate!
Even Rover gets a turn,
His slobber makes my stomach churn.

So deck the holly, light the tree,
But keep that mistletoe from me!

Colin Harrison

Father UnChristmas

I'm Father UnChristmas
And I curse and I grouse
As I squirm through your keyhole
To de-Santa your house.

I rip up the trimmings;
Break the bulbs in the lights;
In your stocking you'll find
A serpent that bites . . .
  From a time of goodwill
  I make a season of frights!

In their boxes, the chocolates
Are turned into stones.
I bring a sack of old worries
And bags of new moans.
  From a time of goodwill
  I make a season of groans.

I'm Father UnChristmas
And I curse and I grouse
As I squirm through your keyhole
To de-Santa your house.

Trevor Millum

Superhero Santa

Santa said, at his Arctic base,
'I'll make this world a better place.'

Now Super Santa – zap, pow, thwack –
socks nasty no-goods with his sack.
Who would have thought so many toys,
unclaimed by naughty girls and boys,
would have made the perfect tool
to stop street crime? Santa Rules!

Flying reindeer cut down time
it takes to get to any crime:
sweet stealers, dodgy comic dealers,
have zero chance. Hear those squealers:
'Super Santa – zap, pow, thwack –
socked us all with his mighty sack.'

Yes, Super Santa (plus his pixies),
helps good people, when in fixes.

Mike Johnson

Christmas Worm 3

Wow!' said the worm,
'this soil tastes good,'
as she burrowed her way
through the Christmas pud.

Tony Mitton

Greetings from Planet Christmas

It was after the Christmas party.
We'd had crisps, sandwiches, cakes and all that stuff
And Santa Claus had been with the prezzies.
'Quick!' said Mum. 'Let's go outside.
We might see him take off from the roof and zoom into the night sky.'
As if!
Still, we all rushed out just to humour her.
But something was there, hovering over the chimney.
It wasn't a sleigh with reindeer, piled high with toys.
It was a space ship.
It was!
It was shaped like a rugby ball
flashing with lights
humming like a thousand bees.
A door zipped open and a set of steps slid down to the tiles.
All those little aliens appeared, dressed in red with white edging.
Lots of lIttle Santas.

They were talking in a high-pitched wibble like a cassette played
too fast.
They came down the steps.
Then our Santa popped up through the skylight with his sack on
his back
giving it 'Ho, ho, ho!'
When he saw what was waiting for him he said, 'What the . . . '
and tried to go back, but it was too late.
They grabbed him and pulled him towards the ship.
'Let go!' he shouted. 'Get off me!'
But it was no good, there were too many of them.
They were really excited now. So was my mum.
'Stop it!' she yelled. 'You can't do this. I'll call the police.'
It was no good. They'd got him inside by this time and shut
the door.
Was he their leader or something? Why didn't he want to go?
I went in the house to tell my dad.
He wasn't in the living room.
He wasn't in the kitchen
or the bedroom
or the bathroom.
'Dad!' I shouted. 'Dad!'
Silence.
I couldn't find him anywhere.

Gus Grenfell

I Don't Believe In . . .

I don't believe in custard.
I don't believe in sums.
I don't believe in tonsils.
I don't believe in plums.
I don't believe in aliens
Beyond the Milky Way,
    But I do believe in Santa Claus
    Flying on his sleigh.

I don't believe in thunder.
I don't believe in germs.
I don't believe in Wednesdays.
I don't believe in worms.
I don't believe in nightmares.
I don't believe in snores,
    But I do believe in Christmas
    And good old Santa Claus.

Celia Warren

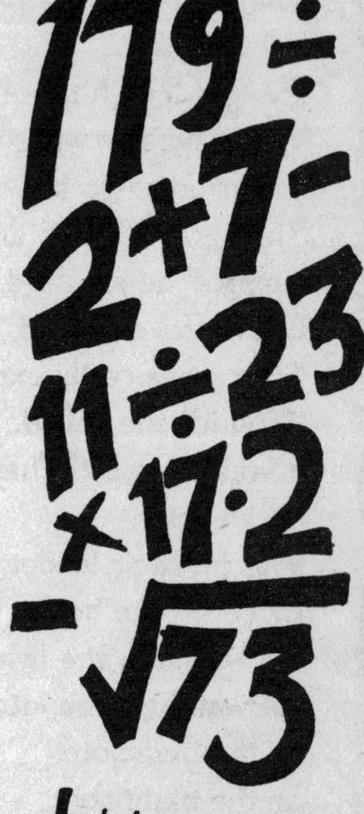

BADOOM
CHARLIE'S
ROOM

Turkey Stuffing

We took out some crumbs for the birds
while the dinner was cooking.
The turkey followed us out
and ate them all when we weren't looking.

Jill Townsend

Christmas Worm 4

'Ooh, look!' said the worm
with a cry of delight.
'Goodness gracious!
The world's turned white.'

Tony Mitton

Our Family's Taking-back Christmas Shopping List!

A winter coat – too big, too colourful,
too expensive,

a bow and arrow –
admired it, fired it,
retired it,

a pocket game – wouldn't work,
wouldn't fit in my pocket,

a digital watch – dead
battery, dead beat,
dead loss,

a radio controlled car – zoomed out
of control, zoomed out of the window,

a new computer – slight hitch,
broken switch,

a moving doll – turned
it on, head fell off,
turned it off,

a pair of tights – kept
snagging, kept sagging,

a mountain bike –
brakes slammed on,
brakes jammed on,

a new jacket – not right, too
bright, too tight,

a football kit – not City,
such a pity,

a pair of socks – too small,
two left feet.

And if Santa had been around we would have taken *him* back

or on second thoughts perhaps we would have given him the *sack*!

Ian Souter

Miss Misery Witch Waits For Santa

Instead of my stocking,
I've hung up my bat.
I'll enjoy watching Santa
try filling that!

I've left out a glass
of 'medicine' tonight.
If he takes a swig
he'll run all through the night . . .

There's a fire in the hearth
   if he comes in that way –
and my pet crocodile
   will be waiting to play.

I've arranged for No Parking
   on all of the roofs
and when he gets back to Rudolf
   . . . there'll be clamps on his hoofs.

Trevor Millum

Riddles For Christmas

The Joke's On You

What is inside me
is of most interest,
though groans often follow
what is revealed.
You need to have pull
to discover my secrets
and earplugs might be
a good idea.

Food For Thought

Born to die
on a famous birthday
yet remembered every day
in one country.
My influence is strong
on all who tackle me;
becoming as one
in a glut of gobbling.

Look Who's Talking

All year long
we look forward
to our night
on the tiles.
Dodgy if
there's a frost.
Seasonal if
there is snow.
Let's hope it
doesn't rain, dear.

John C. Desmond

Answers: cracker, turkey and reindeer

Christmas Pudding

It lay on the table
proudly displayed.
'The best Christmas pudding,'
said Mum, 'ever made.

'You'll all find out
just how good in a minute,
for I've put some special
ingredients in it.'

It did seem sort
of strange somehow.
I couldn't quite
describe it now –

like something from
the fourth dimension.
'It is,' said Mum,
'my own invention.

'You'll all remember
this – don't doubt it!'
Gran peered. 'There's something
odd about it.'

'Well, here we go,'
smiled Mum with pride
and grasped the knife
that lay beside.

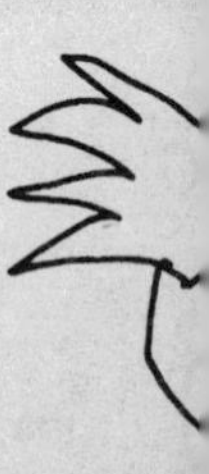

'This is how puddings
should be made.'
The candlelight
gleamed off the blade.

There was a hush.
Time seemed to stop.
The knife blade touched
the pudding top.

The room shook in
a blinding flash,
a huge bang
and a mighty crash.

'Aliens!' I thought.
'Is my laser loaded?'
But no – the pudding
had exploded.

We sat there stunned
in frozen poses.
Bits of it
were up our noses.

Mum looked very
close to tears.
Bits of it
were in our ears.

Bits of it
dropped down the chair.
Bits of it
were in our hair.

Still no one moved
from where we sat.
Bits of it
were on the cat.

'Well then,' said Dad,
'no need to wait.'
Yes – bits of it
were on each plate.

'You're right, dear. Each
year in December,
this is a dish
that we'll remember.'

Bits covered the table
like lumpy lacquer.
'Very clever – a Christmas
pudding cracker.'

Charles Thomson

The Wrong Words

We like to sing the wrong words
to Christmas Carols . . .

We three kings of Orient are,
One in a taxi, one in a car . . .

It drives our music teacher barmy,
his face turns red as a holly berry,
his forehead creases, his eyes bulge.
It looks as if the top of his head
is about to lift like a saucepan lid
as he boils over . . .

His anger spills out
in an almighty shout . . .

'NO.' He roars . . .

'If you do that once more
I'll give you the kind of Christmas gift
you won't forget in a hurry . . .'

So we sing . . .

. . . most highly flavoured lady . . .

'IT'S FAVOURED,' he screams
'NOT FLAVOURED . . .

'What do you think she is,
an ice cream cone?'

Then, to cap it all,
and drive him really wild
we sing of the shepherds
washing their socks,
till he slams down the piano lid
and takes off like a rocket
into the stratosphere,
lighting up the sky
like a Christmas star.

Brian Moses

The Day After The Day After Boxing Day

On the day after the day after Boxing Day
Santa wakes up, eventually,
puts away his big red suit and wellies,
lets Rudolph and the gang out into the meadow
then shaves his head and beard.

He puts on his new cool sunglasses,
baggy blue Bermuda shorts (he's sick of red),
yellow stripy T-shirt that doesn't quite cover his belly
and lets his toes breathe in flip-flops.

Packing a bucket and spade,
fifteen tubes of Factor Twenty suncream
and seventeen romantic novels
he fills his Walkman with the latest sounds,
is glad to use a proper suitcase instead of the old sack
and heads off into the Mediterranean sunrise
enjoying the comforts of a Boeing 747
(although he passes on the free drinks).

Six months later,
relaxed, red and a little more than stubbly,
he looks at his watch, adjusts his wide-brimmed sunhat,
mops the sweat from his brow and strokes his chin,
wondering why holidays always seem to go so quickly.

Paul Cookson

Polar Bears and Penguins

Polar bears and penguins
Playing in the snow;
You see them on your Christmas cards,
But don't the artists know
That polar bears live *northwards*
In the Arctic all the year,
And penguins only hang out
In the *southern* hemisphere!

So listen, all you artists,
You're making me uptight;
THEY NEVER MEET EACH OTHER
So get it flippin' right!

Mike Jubb

I'VE NEVER MET A POLAR BEAR
NOR ME
ME NEITHER

Present from Aunty

I open my present
in a rush.
Just what I wanted –
a toilet brush.

Thank you, Aunty,
that's ever so nice,
but, look here, I
can see the price.

A bargain brush –
99p.
You bought it specially
for me.

You know I've always
wanted one.
I'm sure that I'll
have hours of fun.

I just can't wait
to get it rubbing,
plunging, scraping,
stabbing, scrubbing.

For now, I'll put it
over here
by the sink plunger
I got last year.

Charles Thomson

Christmas Capers

Kelly Clarke, Kelly Clarke,
Always ready for a lark,
Took apart the Christmas tree,
Wolfed the chocolate mice with glee.

Tied the tinsel to the cat,
Squashed the fluffy robin flat,
Undid all the velvet bows,
Cut off Rudolph's shiny nose.

Cracked the crackers, popped the poppers,
Broke the sparkling crystal droppers,
Took the clangers from the bells,
Stripped the merry Christmas elves.

Then, remembering past fights,
Unhooked the pretty fairy lights,
Wrapped them round her little sister,
Plugged them in, and up she lit her!

Patricia Leighton

Whodunnit?

It's the night before Christmas
And – oh, dear me!
Something has eaten
The Christmas tree!

It hasn't a needle,
It hasn't a pin,
Just fat tinsel caterpillars
Wearing a grin!

Sue Cowling

Christmas Worm 5

'See you next year,'
said the worm with a sigh,
as she snuggled to sleep
in a stale mince pie.

Tony Mitton

WE WAS ROBBED

More football poems chosen by David Orme

Football Through the Ages

Football grew from itchy feet
kicking whatever they found in the street;
a pebble; a stick; a rolling stone;
a rusty can or an animal's bone.
The left-over bladder of a butchered pig,
inflated and tied off, was perfect to kick;
if something would roll it would do for the game
that then had not even been given a name
till, on through the ages, the game was to grow,
at long last becoming the football we know.

O, I'm glad of my football, I'm glad of the rules,
I'm glad of the pitches at clubs and at schools,
I'm glad of my kit, but I am even gladder
the days are long gone when they kicked a pig's bladder.

Celia Warren

MORE SECRET LIVE OF TEACHERS

Poems chosen by Brian Moses

Sir's a Secret Agent

Sir's a secret agent
He's licensed to thrill
At Double-Oh Sevening
He's got bags of skill.

He's tall, dark and handsome
With a muscular frame
Teaching's his profession
But Danger's his game!

He's cool and he's calm
When he makes a decision
He's a pilot, sky-diver
And can teach long-division.

No mission's too big
No mission's too small
School-kids, mad scientists
He takes care of them all.

He sorts out the villains
The spies and the crooks
Then comes back to school
And marks all our books!

Tony Langham

A selected list of poetry books available from Macmillan

The prices shown below are correct at the time of going to press. However, Macmillan Publishers reserve the right to show new retail prices on covers which may differ from those previously advertised.

The Secret Lives of Teachers
Revealing rhymes, chosen by Brian Moses £3.50

'Ere we Go!
Football poems, chosen by David Orme £2.99

You'll Never Walk Alone
More football poems, chosen by David Orme £2.99

Nothing Tastes Quite Like a Gerbil
And other vile verses, chosen by David Orme £2.99

Custard Pie
Poems that are jokes, chosen by Pie Corbett £2.99

Tongue Twisters and Tonsil Twizzlers
Poems chosen by Paul Cookson £2.99

All Macmillan titles can be ordered at your local bookshop or are available by post from:

Book Service by Post
PO Box 29, Douglas, Isle of Man IM99 1BQ

Credit cards accepted. For details:
Telephone: 01624 675137
Fax: 01624 670923
E-mail: bookshop@enterprise.net

Free postage and packing in the UK.
Overseas customers: add £1 per book (paperback) and £3 per book (hardback).